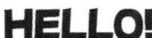

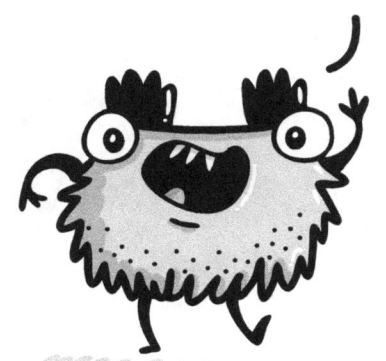

I wanted to say thanks to my
friends Mindy and Kim. Without
the both of you, this book would
still be sitting on my desk.

HOW TO DRAW
SILLY MONSTERS

IT'S SO EASY IT'S SCARY!

BY DZINGEEK

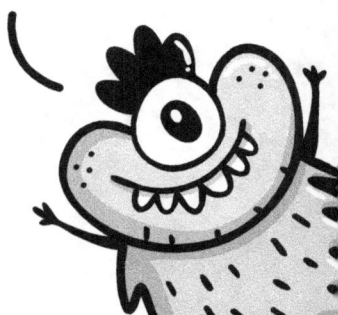

RUSTY CRABCAKES

1.

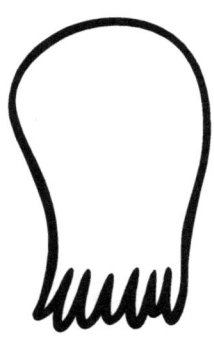

2.

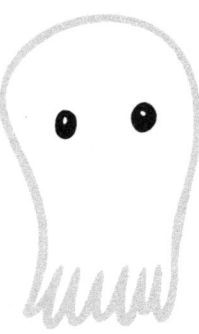

3.

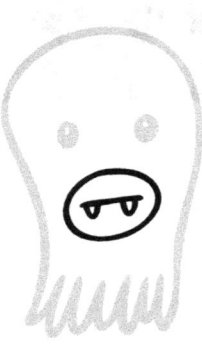

4.

5.

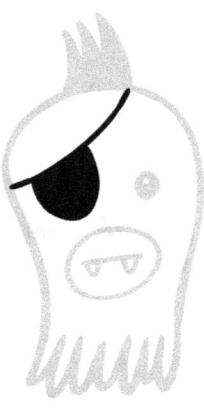

6.

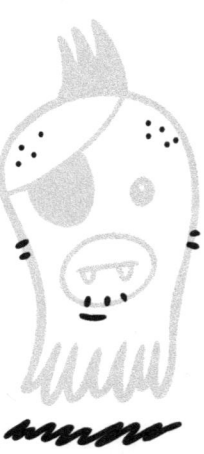

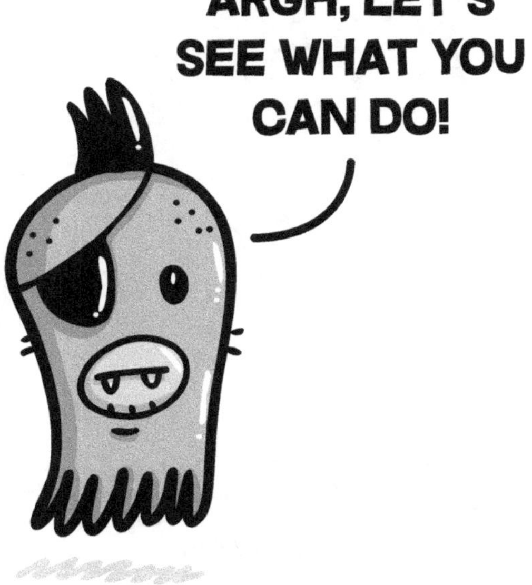
ARGH, LET'S SEE WHAT YOU CAN DO!

TITO DEL FUEGO

1.

2.

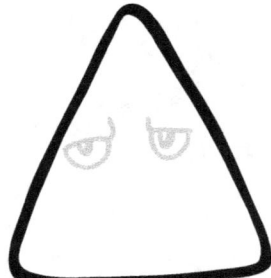

3.

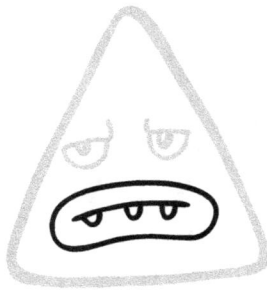

4.

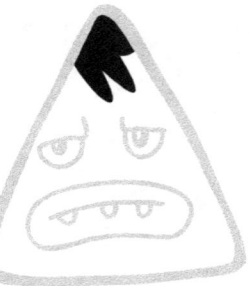

5.

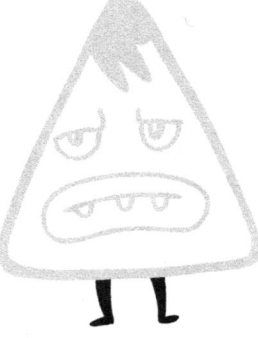

6.

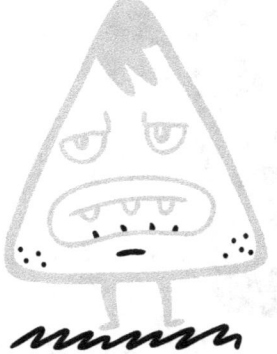

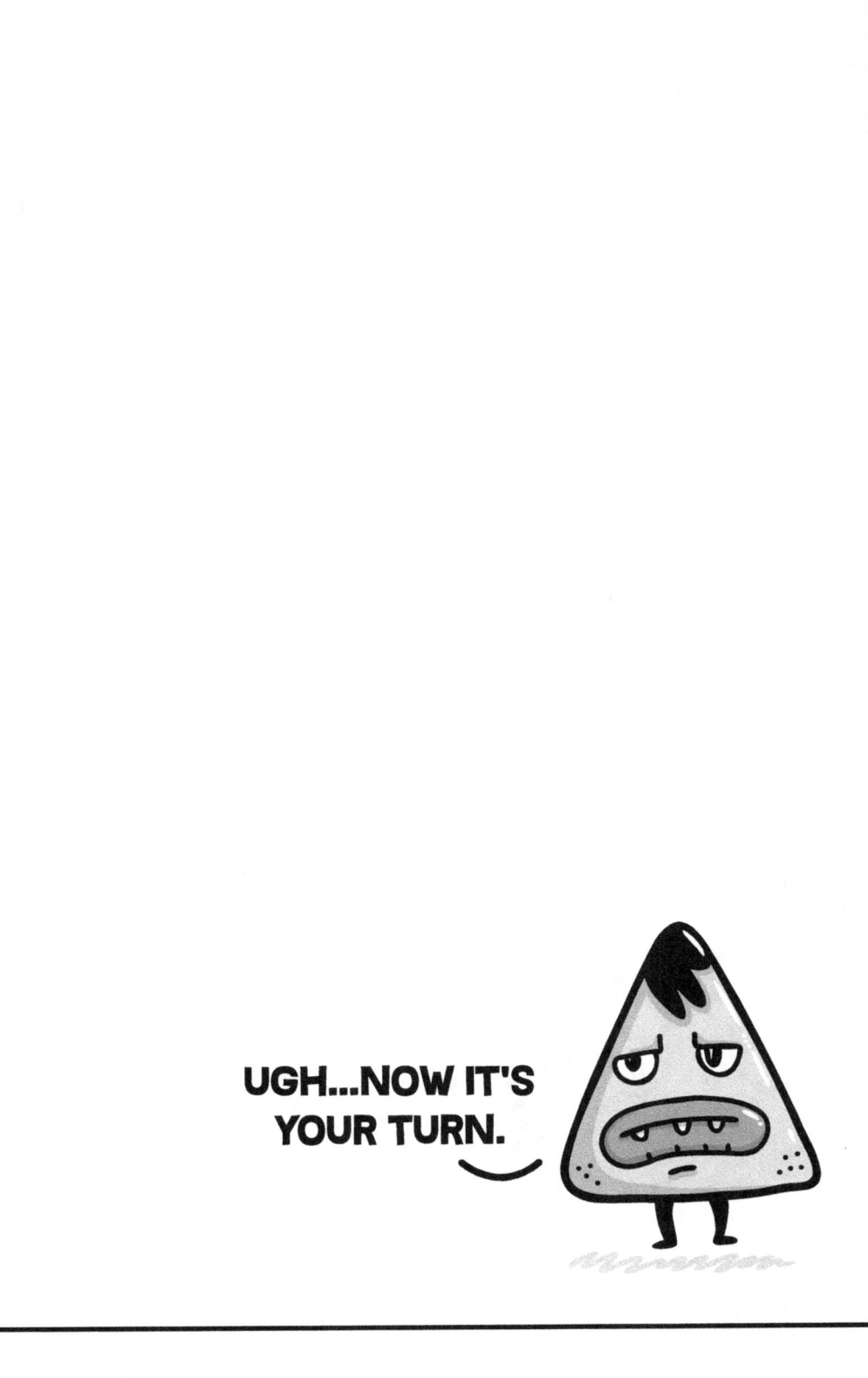

STEVIE BONES

1.

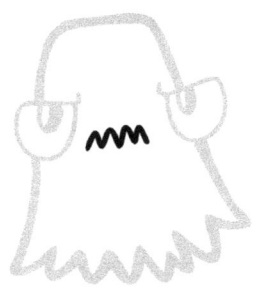

2.

3.

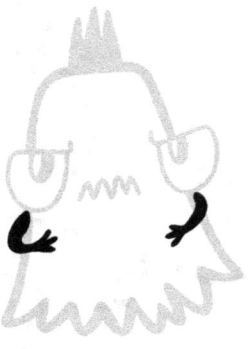

4.

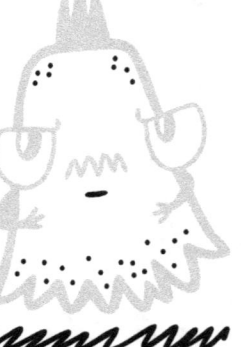

5.

6.

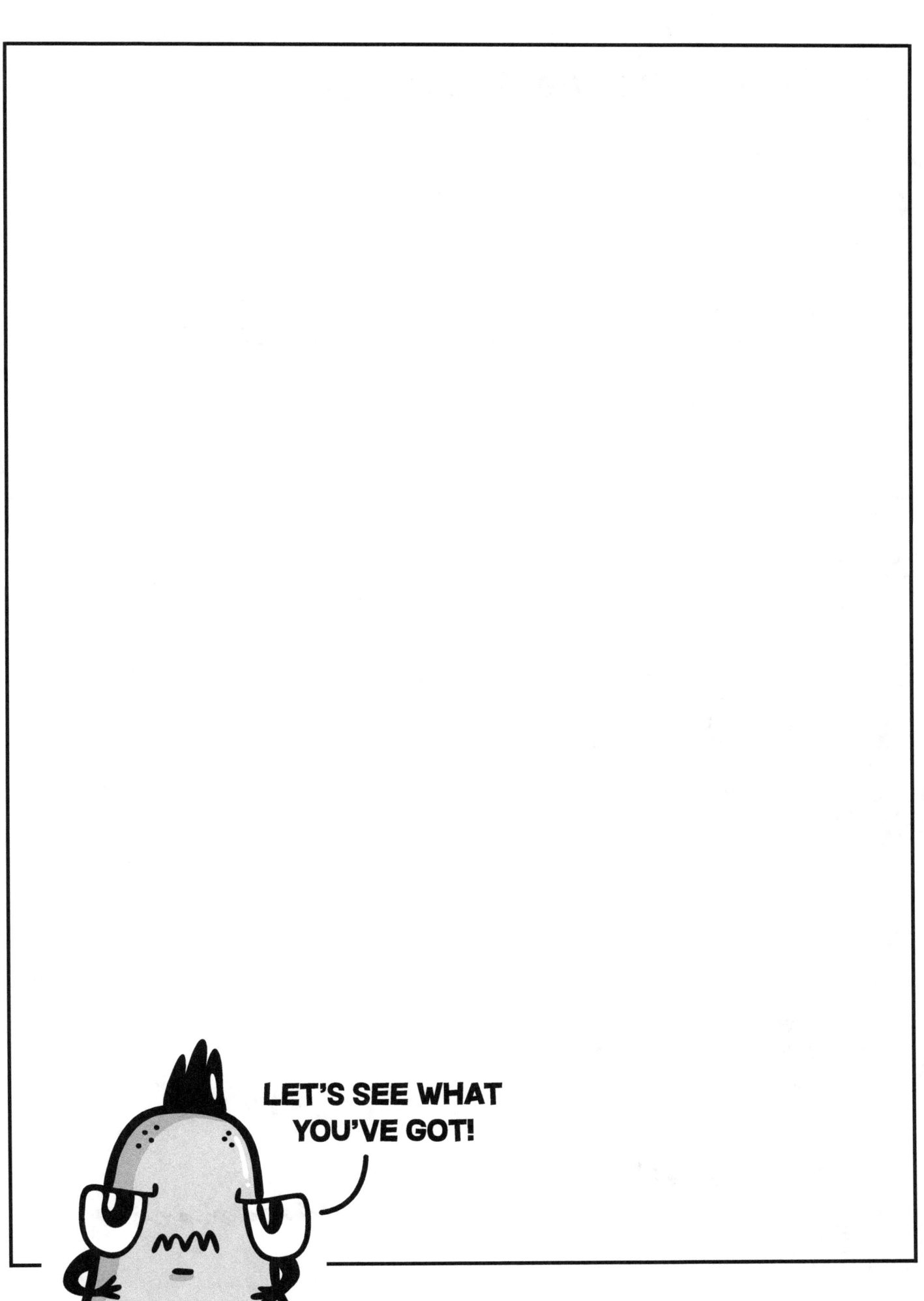

DESEAN MCFLUFFER

1.

2.

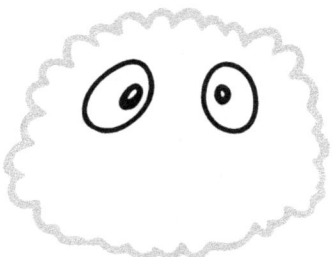

3.

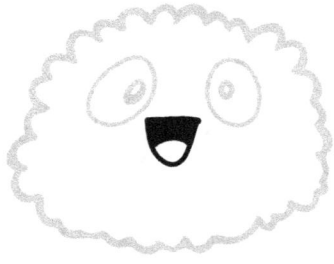

4.

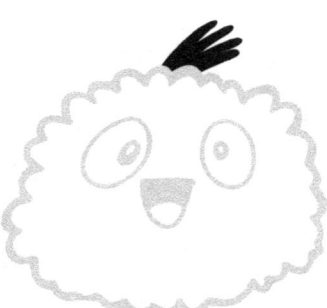

5.

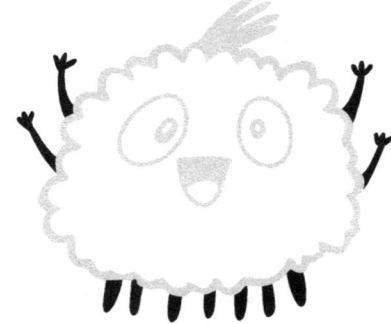

6.

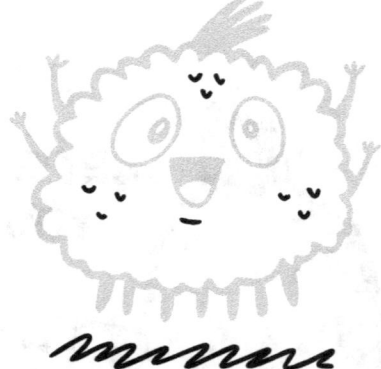

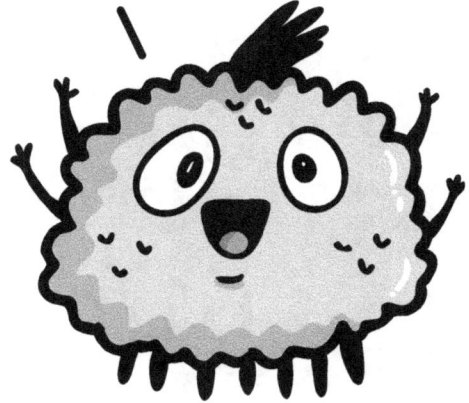

SPIKE LE LOOF

1.

2.

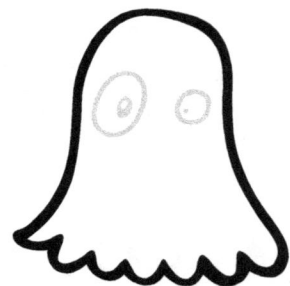

3.

4.

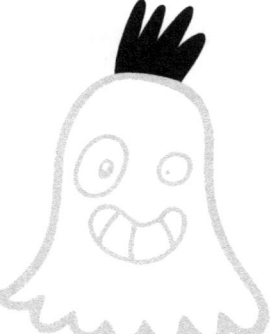

5.

6.

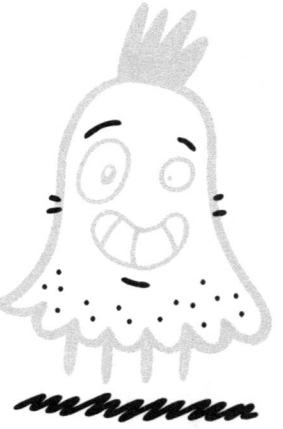

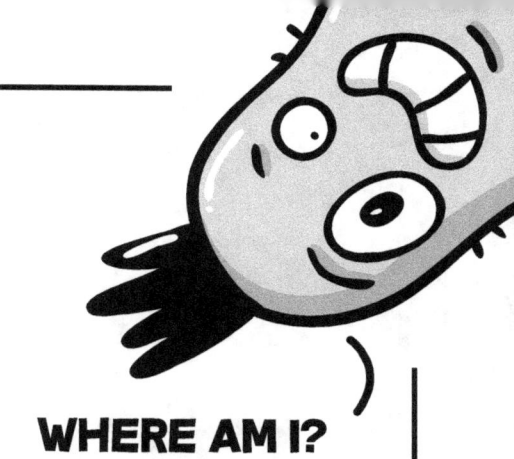

WHERE AM I?

SLIPPERY JONES

1.

2.

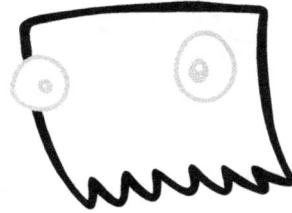

3.

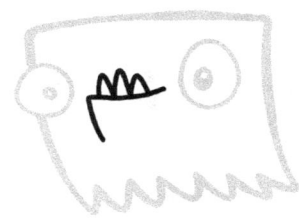

4.

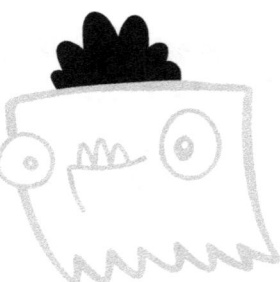

5.

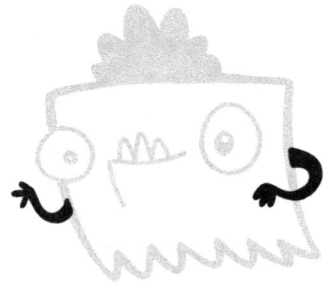

6.

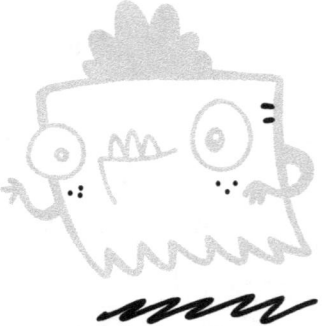

NOW IT'S YOUR
TURN!

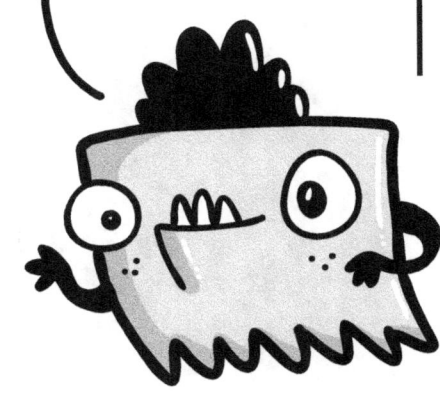

FANG THE GREAT

1.

2.

3.

4.

5.

6.

PENNY PUFFERTON

1.

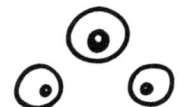

2.

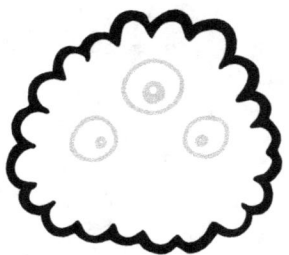

3.

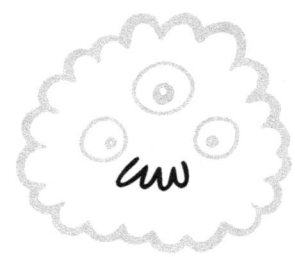

4.

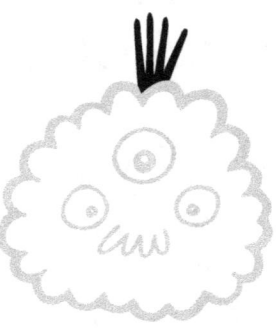

5.

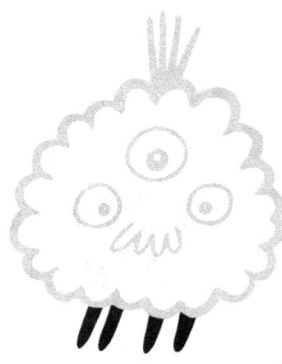

6.

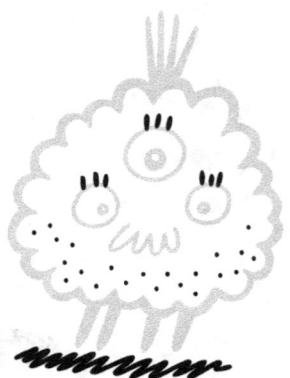

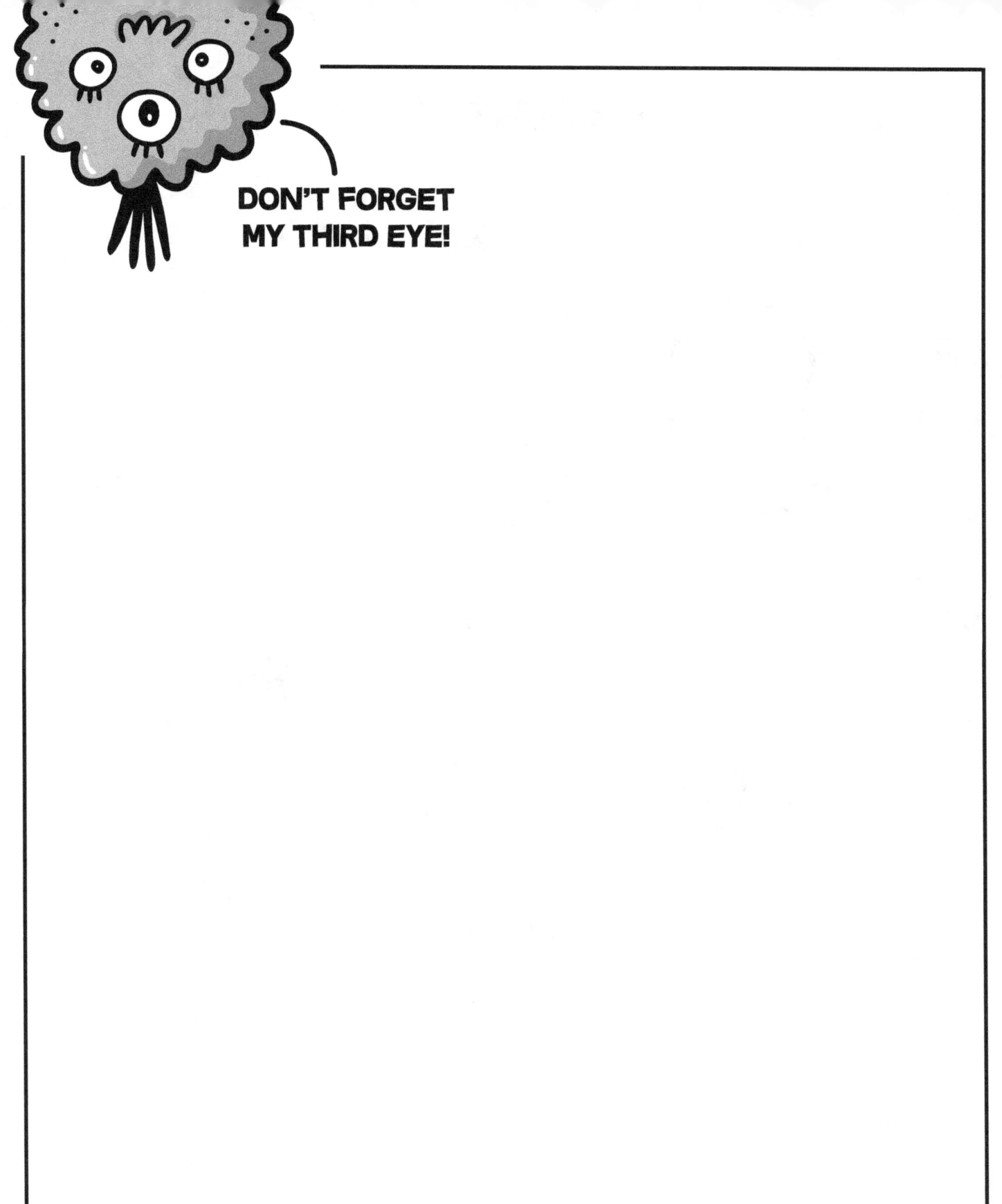

SCREAMIN' MIMI

1.

2.

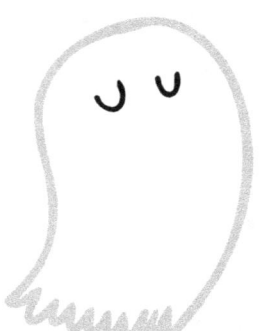

3.

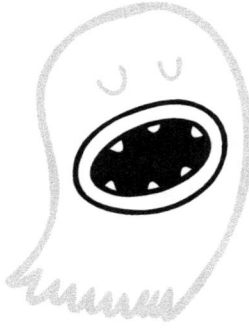

4.

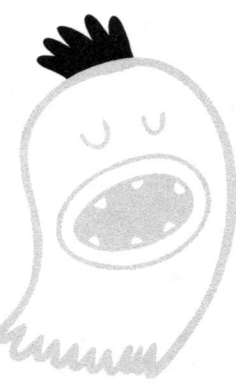

5.

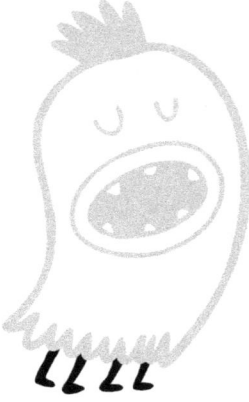

6.

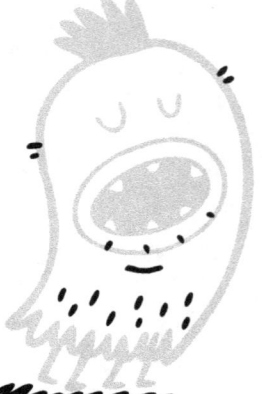

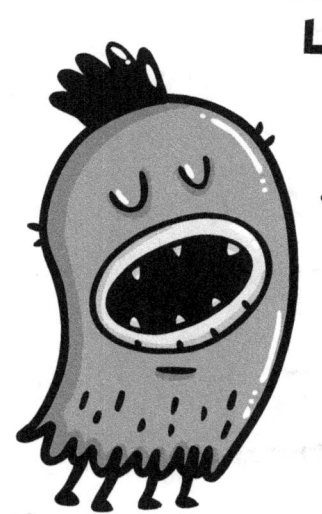

WELL...IT LOOKS
LIKE IT'S YOUR
TURN NOW!

BIG MOUTH TONY

1.

2.

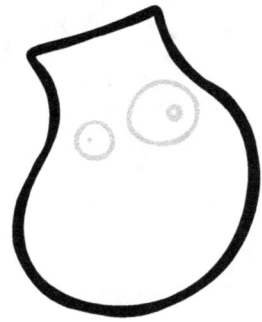

3.

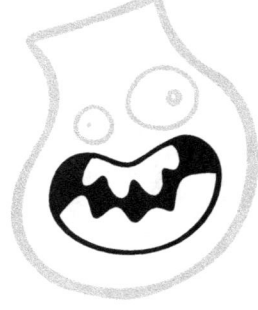

4.

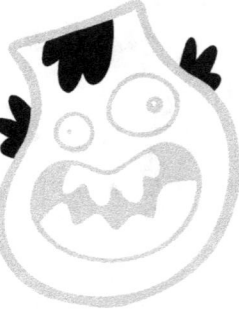

5.

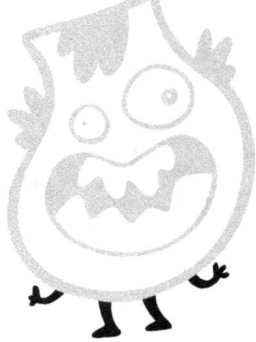

6.

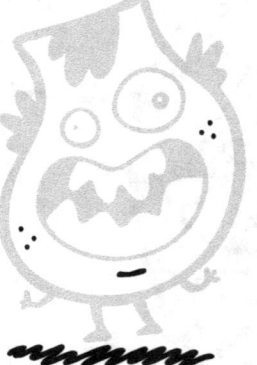

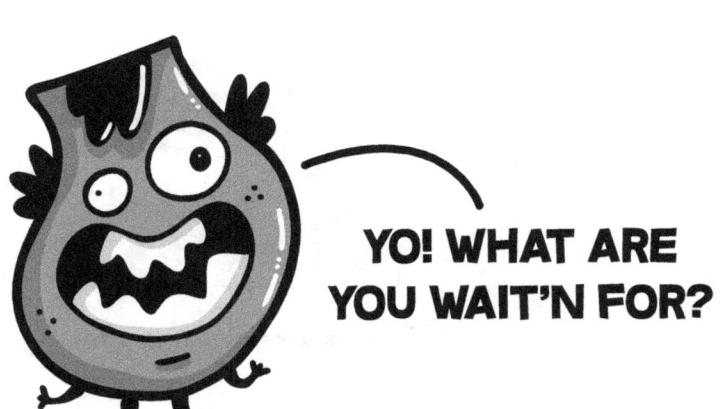

YO! WHAT ARE YOU WAIT'N FOR?

JORGE FLUFFY BEARD

1.

2.

3.

4.

5.

6.
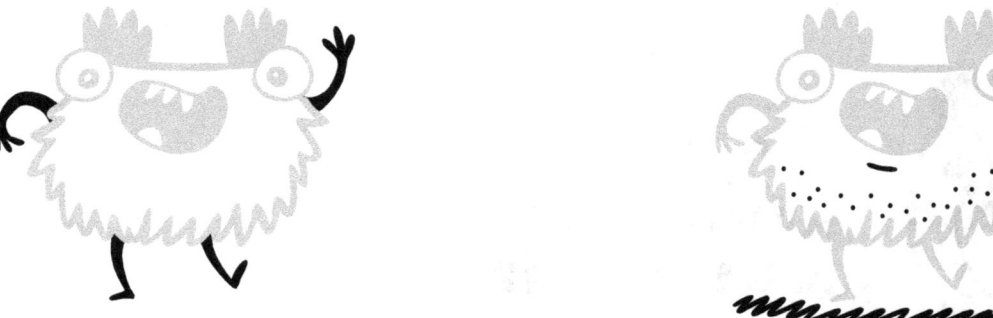

I CAN'T WAIT TO
SEE HOW YOU DO!

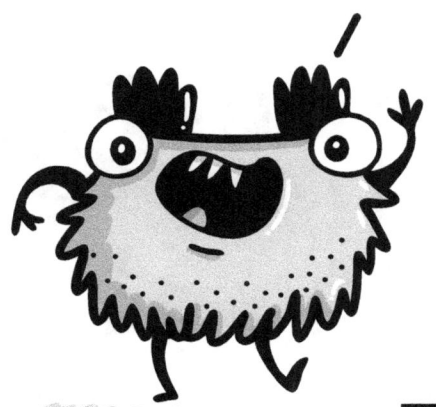

SMELLY ST. ONION

1.

2.

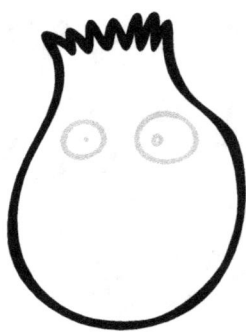

3.

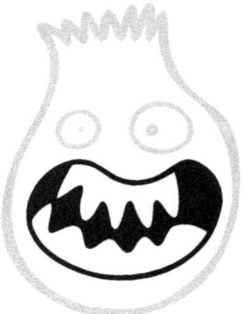

4.

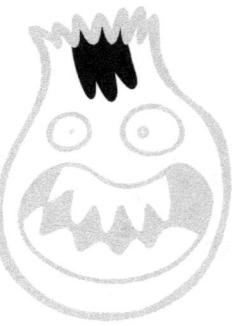

5.

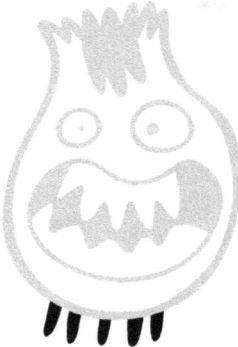

6.

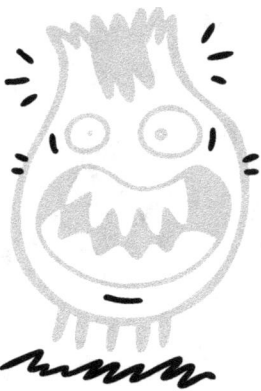

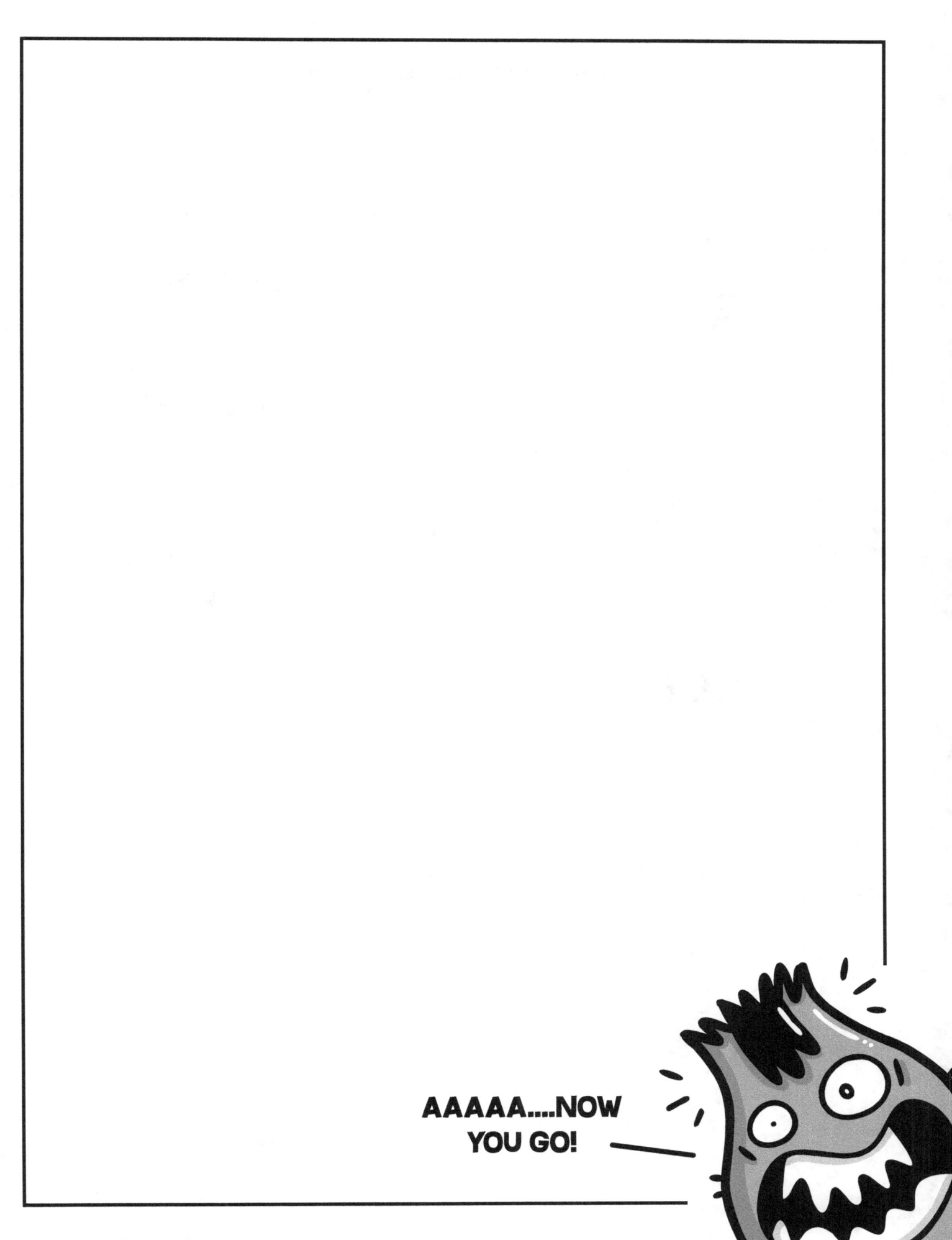

AAAAA....NOW
YOU GO!

FLUFF MCPUFF

1.

2.
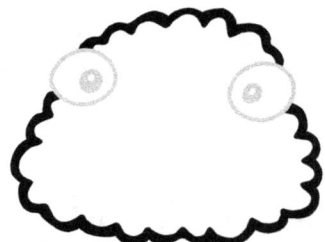

3.
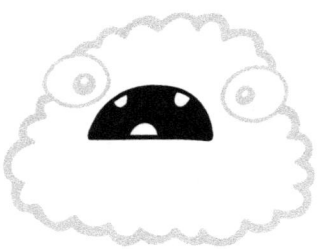

4.
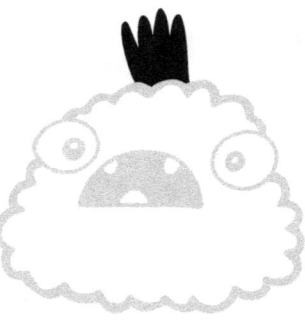

5.
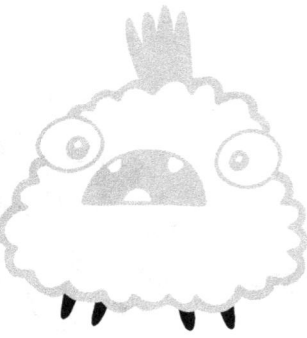

6.
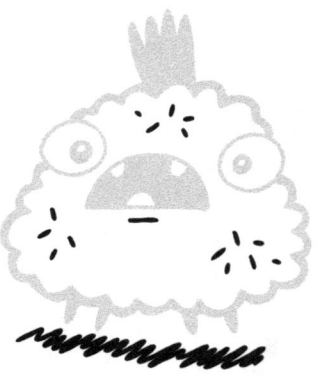

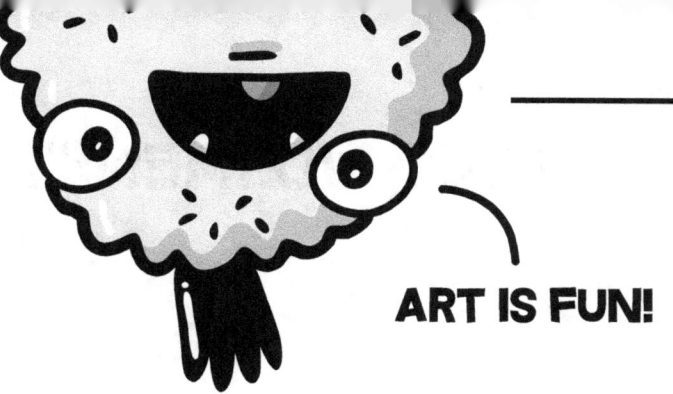

ART IS FUN!

LUCY WORMENSTEIN

1.

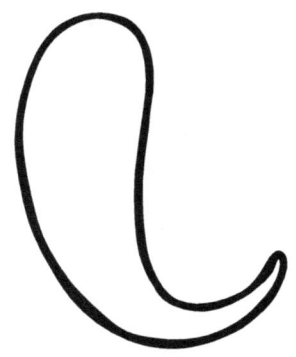

2.

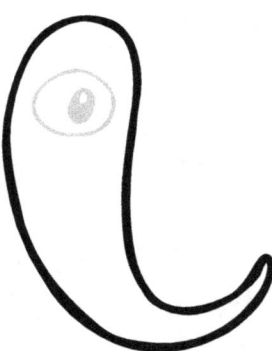

3.

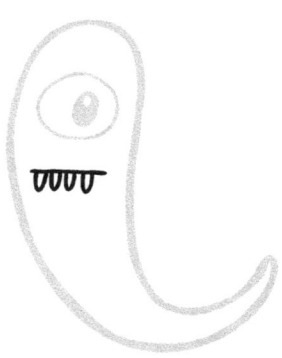

4.

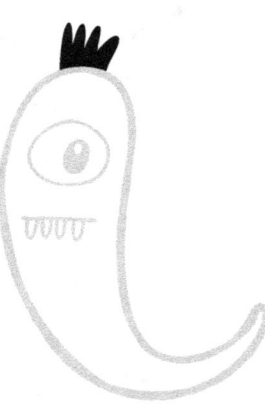

5.

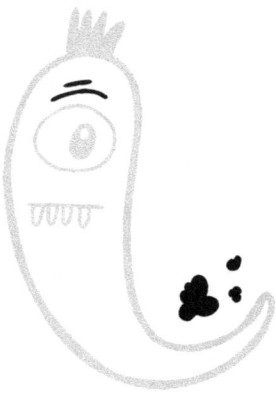

6.

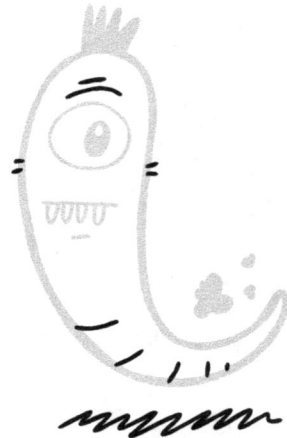

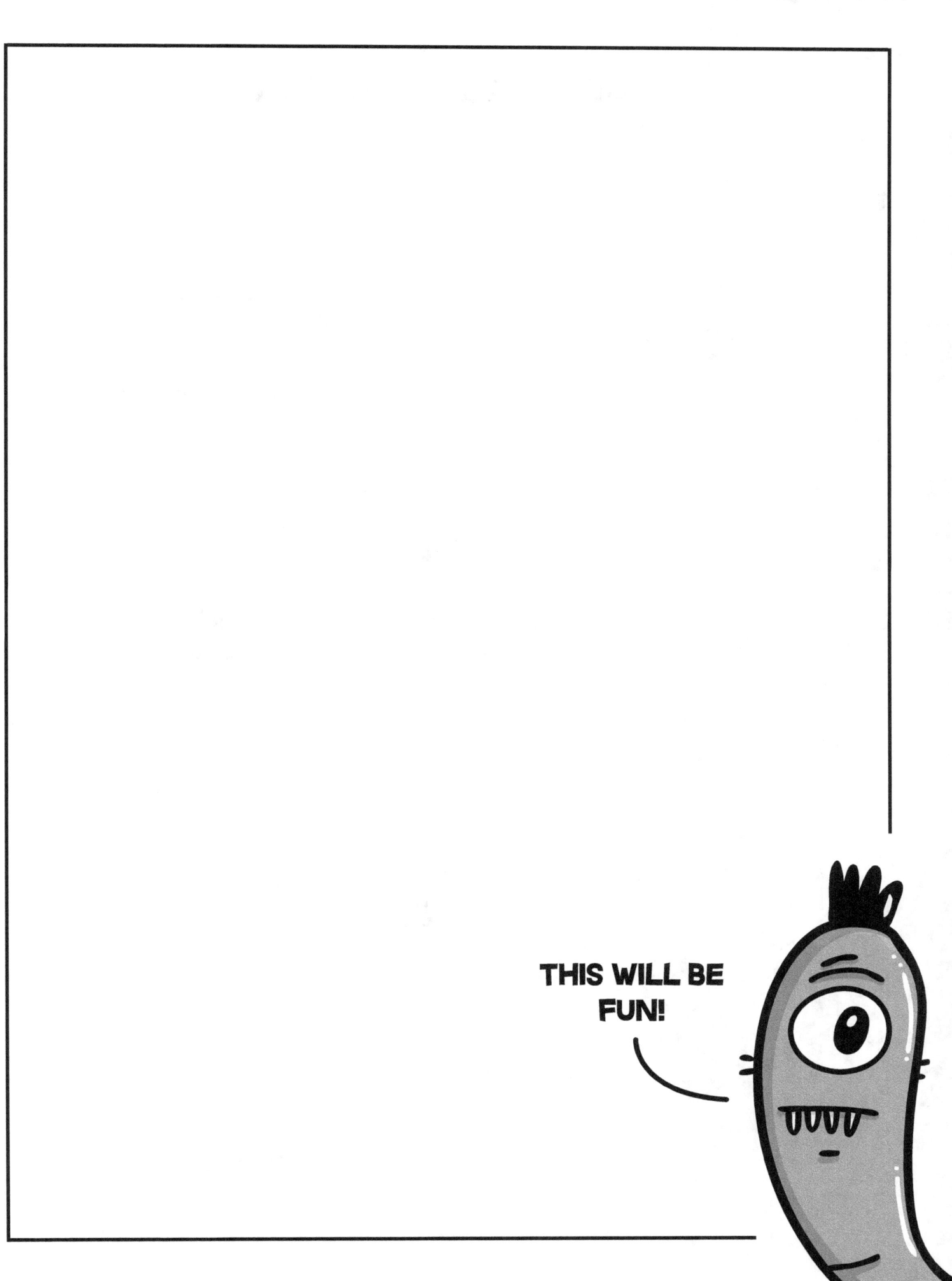

JADE TOOTHINGTON

1.

2.

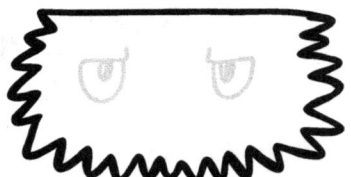

3.

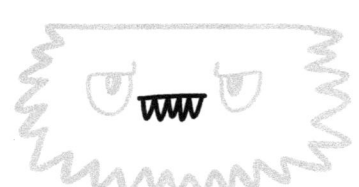

4.

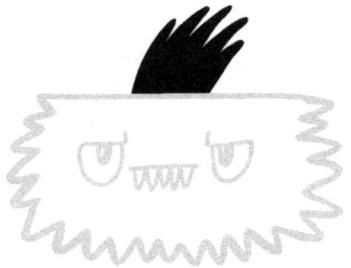

5.

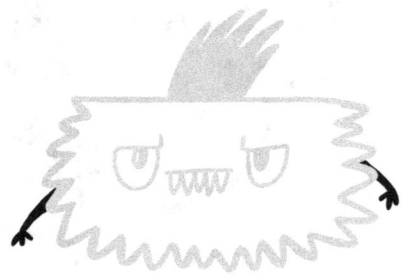

6.

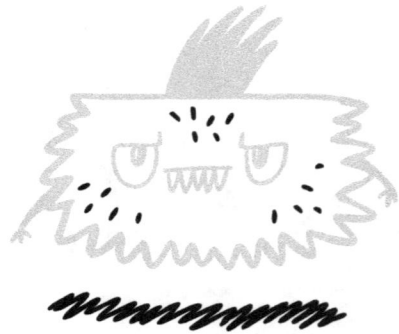

GIVE IT
A TRY!

THE EARL OF UNDERBITE

1.

2.

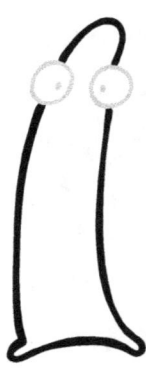

3.

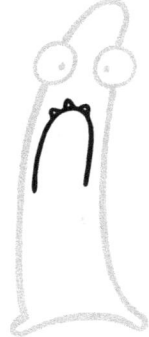

4.

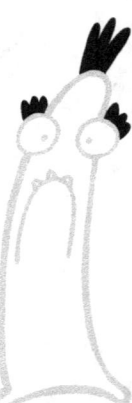

5.

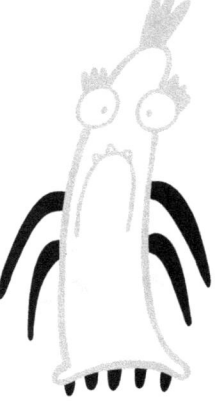

6.

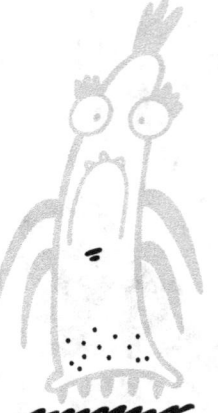

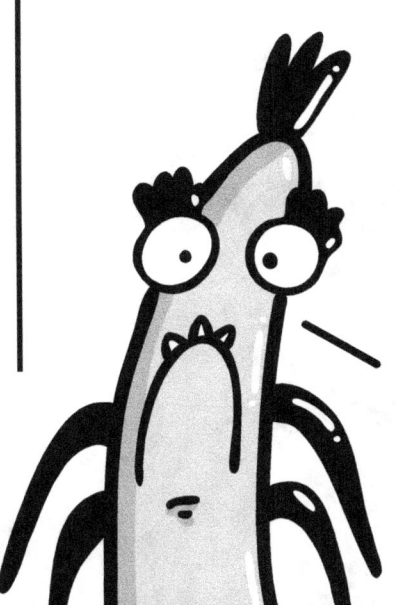

MMM...I WISH I
COULD DRAW.

LEIF HAIR-ICKSON

1.

2.

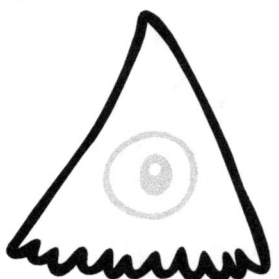

3.

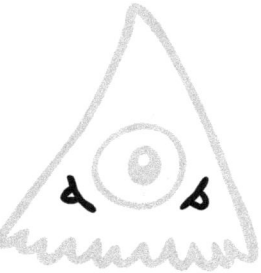

4.

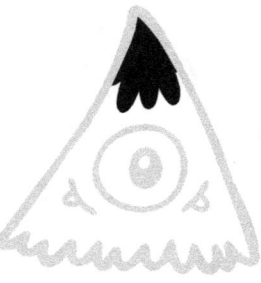

5.

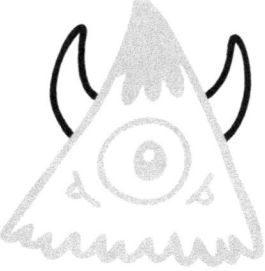

6.

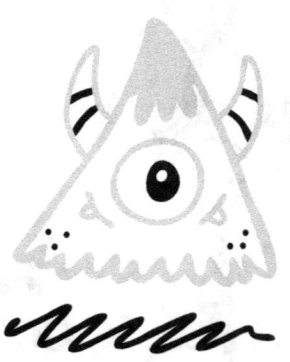

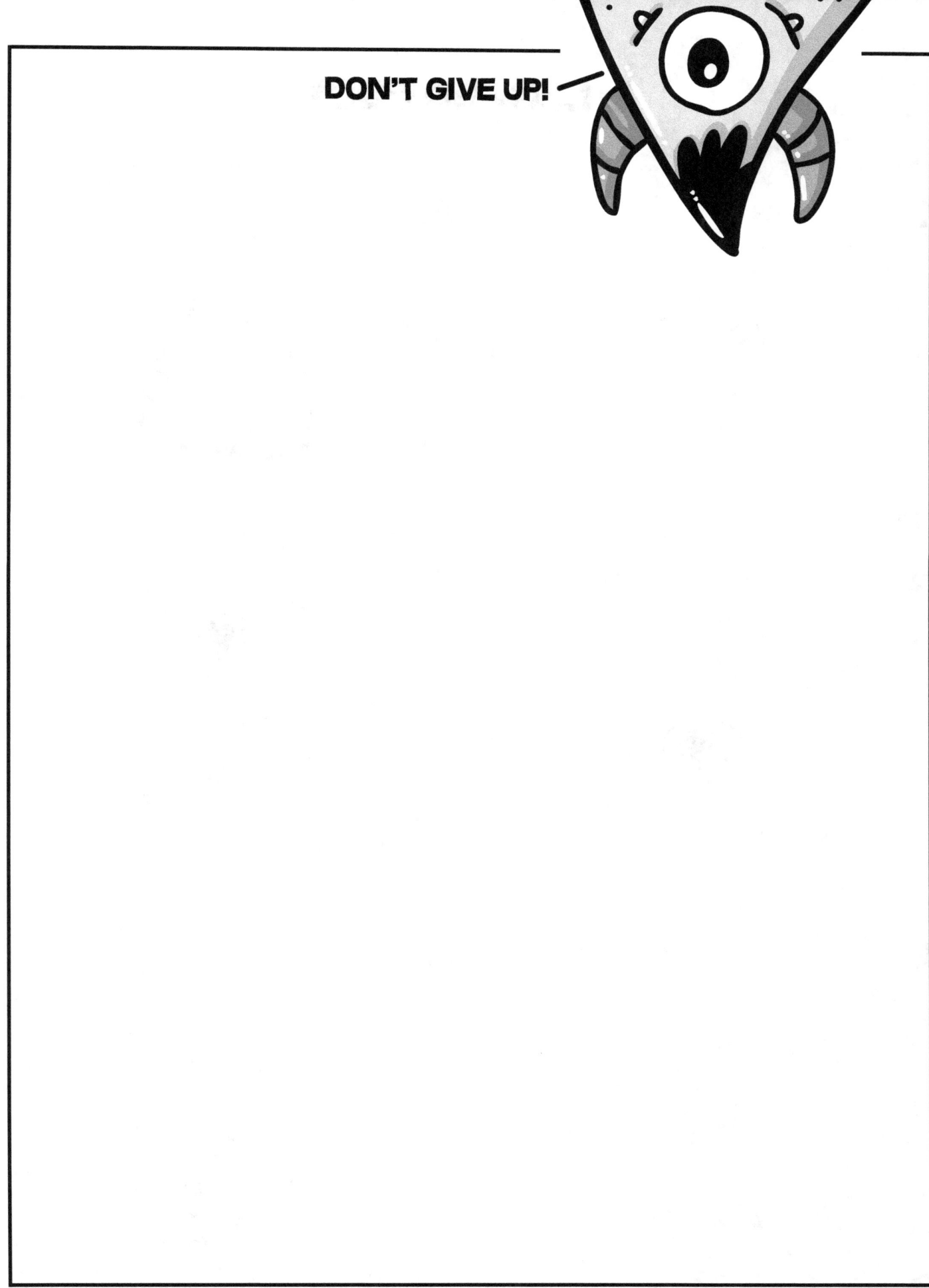

DON'T GIVE UP!

DON'T GIVE UP!

3-LEGGED EDDY

1.

2.

3.

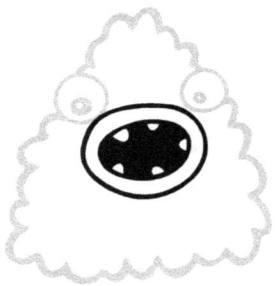

4.

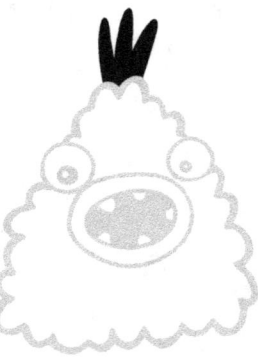

5.

6.

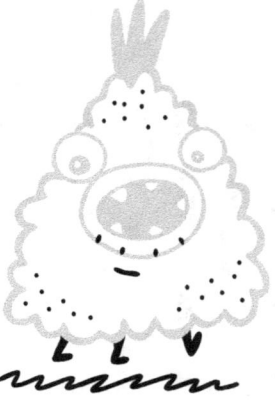

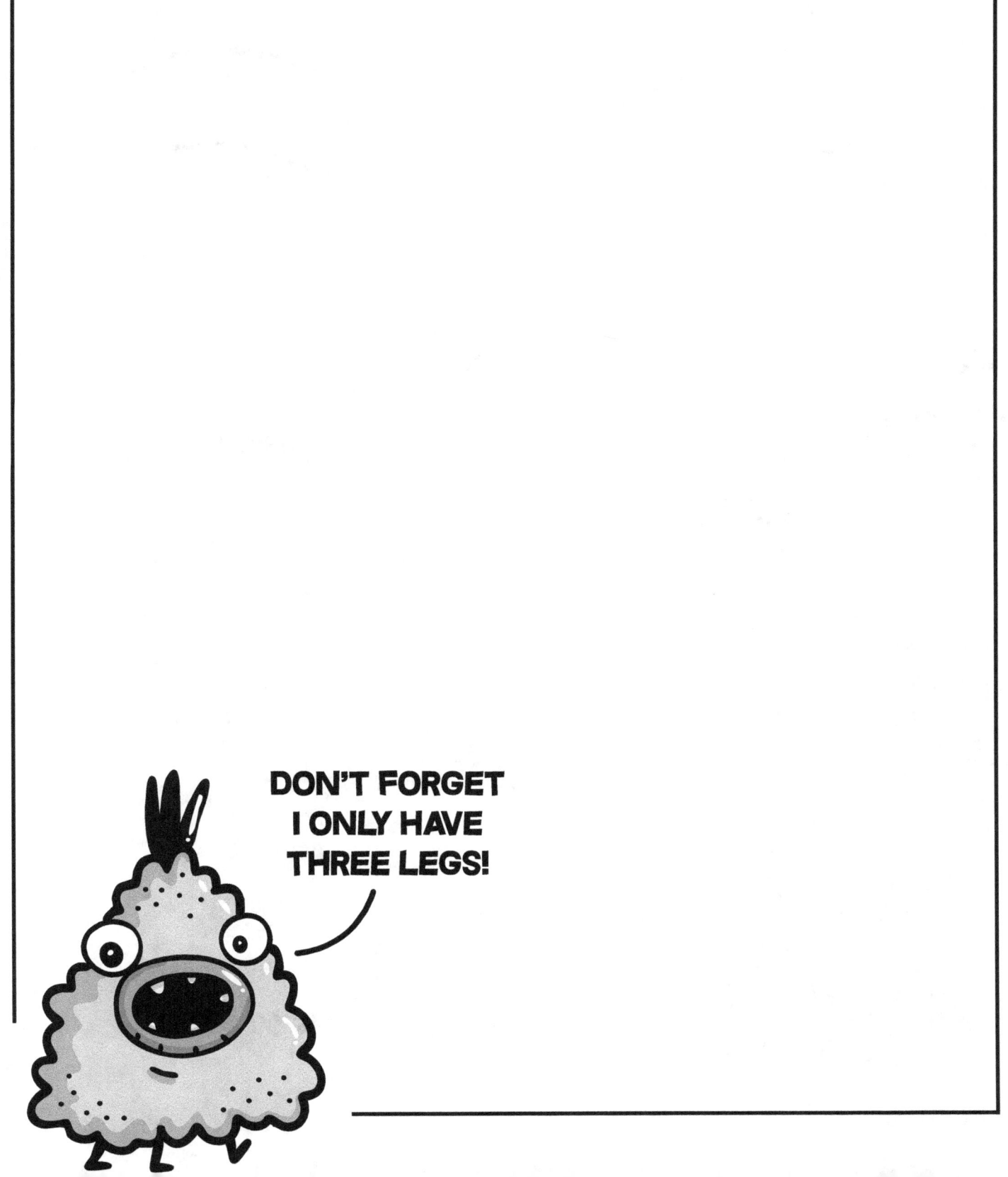

SKIP GOGGLES

1.

2.

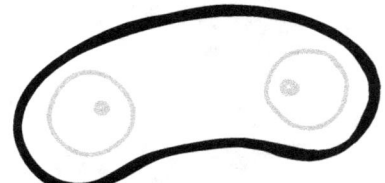

3.

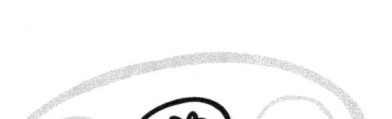

4.

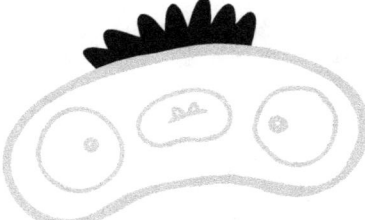

5.

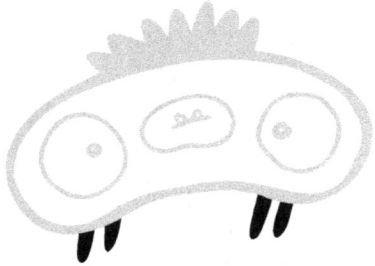

6.

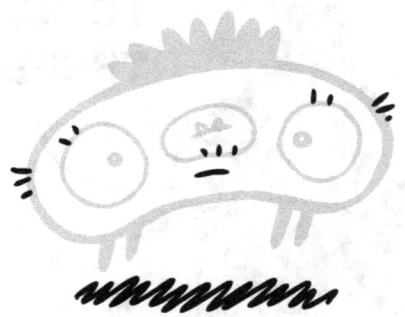

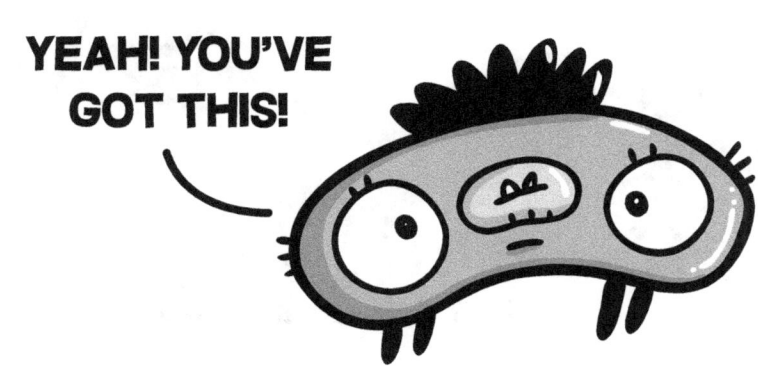

CHIPSWORTH CHARLIE

1.

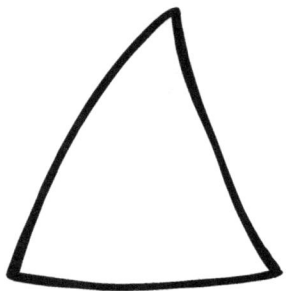

2.

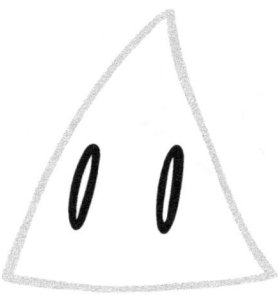

3.

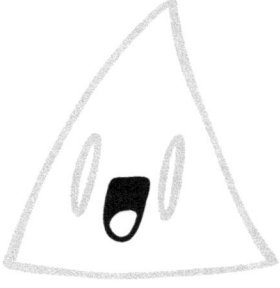

4.

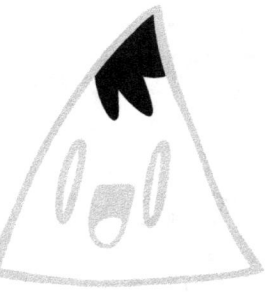

5.

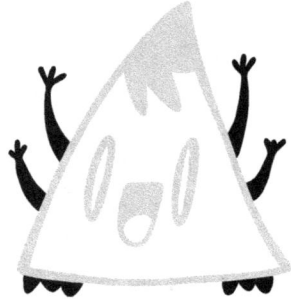

6.

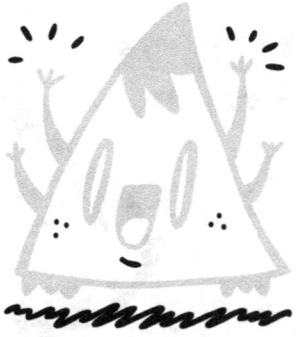

NICE WORK!

SQUIGGLY MCFIGGLE

1.

2.

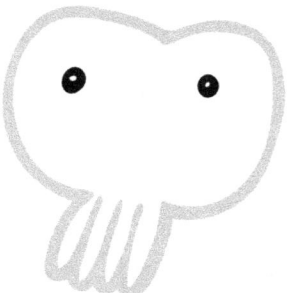

3.

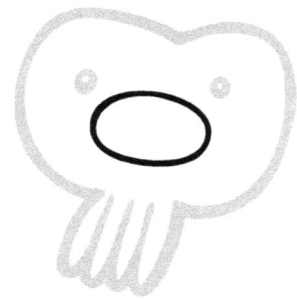

4.

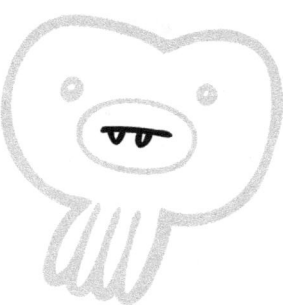

5.

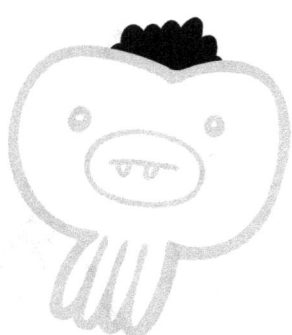

6.

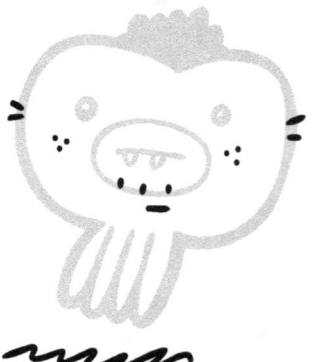

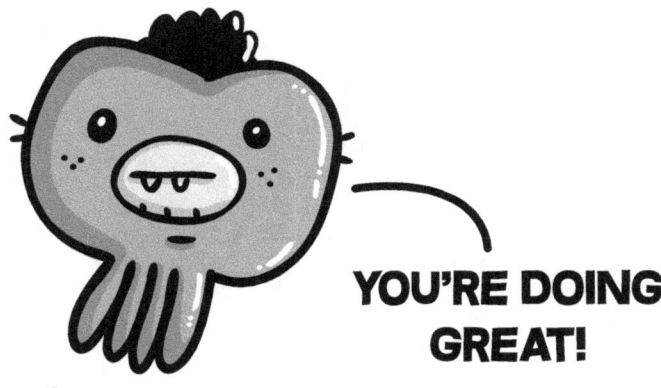

YOU'RE DOING
GREAT!

GREASY SQUISHTOFFERSON

1.

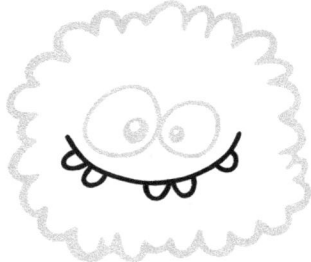

2.

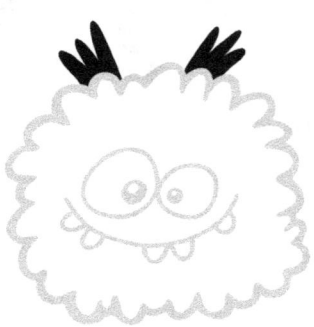

3.

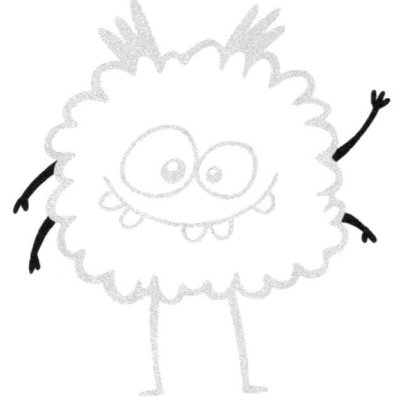

4.

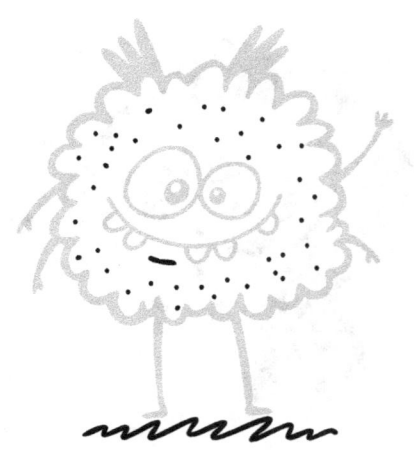

5.

6.

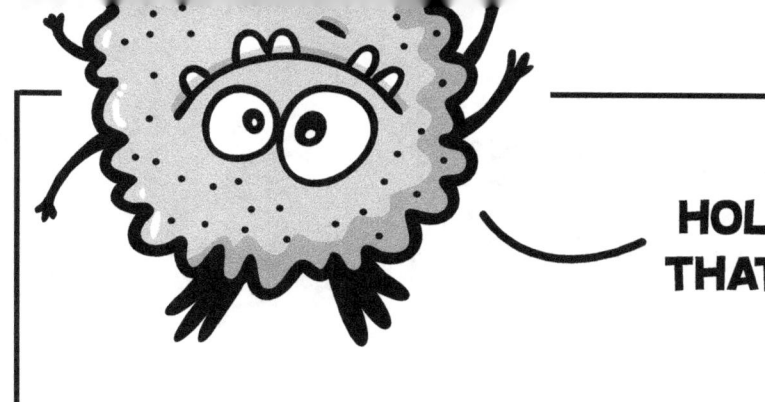

HOLD ON TO
THAT PENCIL!

SCAREDY O'SHEETS

1.

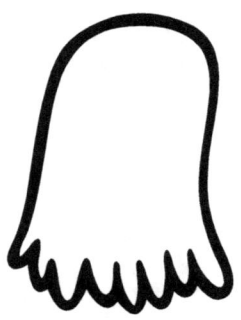

2.

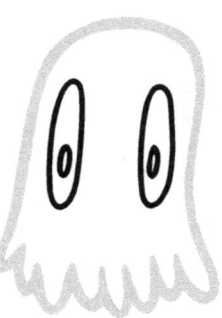

3.

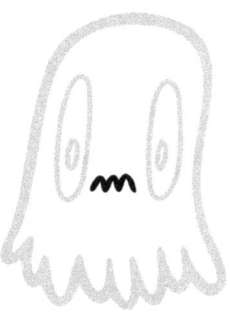

4.

5.

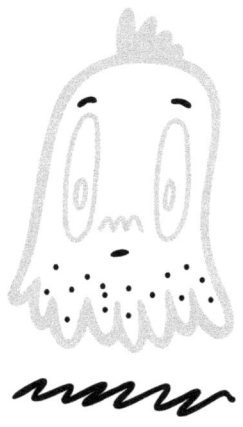

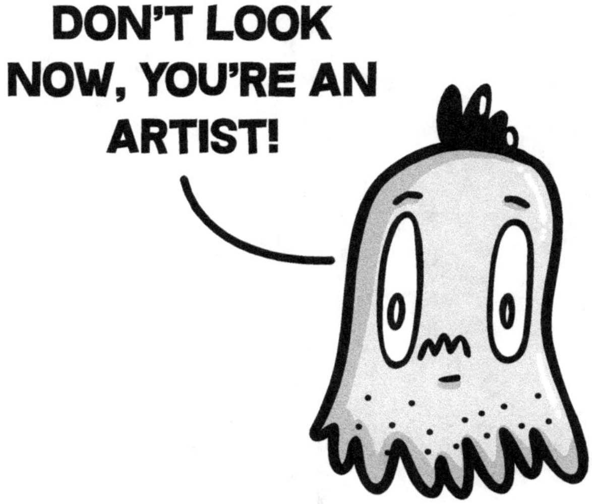
DON'T LOOK NOW, YOU'RE AN ARTIST!

BALLIN' OATS

1.

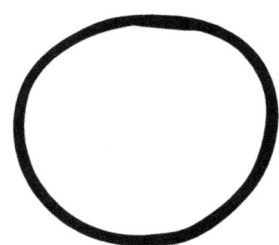

2.

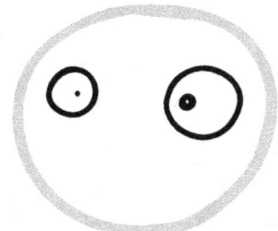

3.

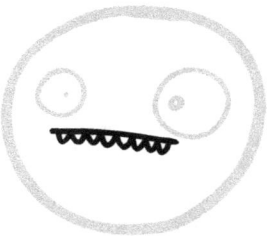

4.

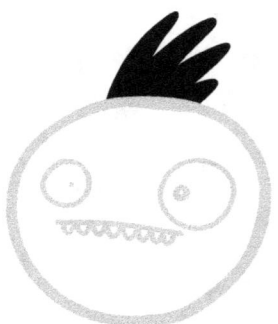

5.

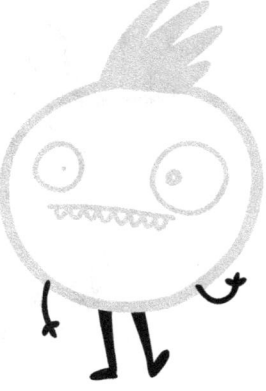

6.

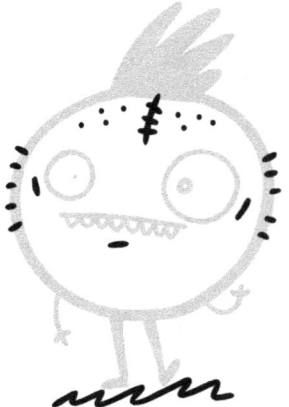

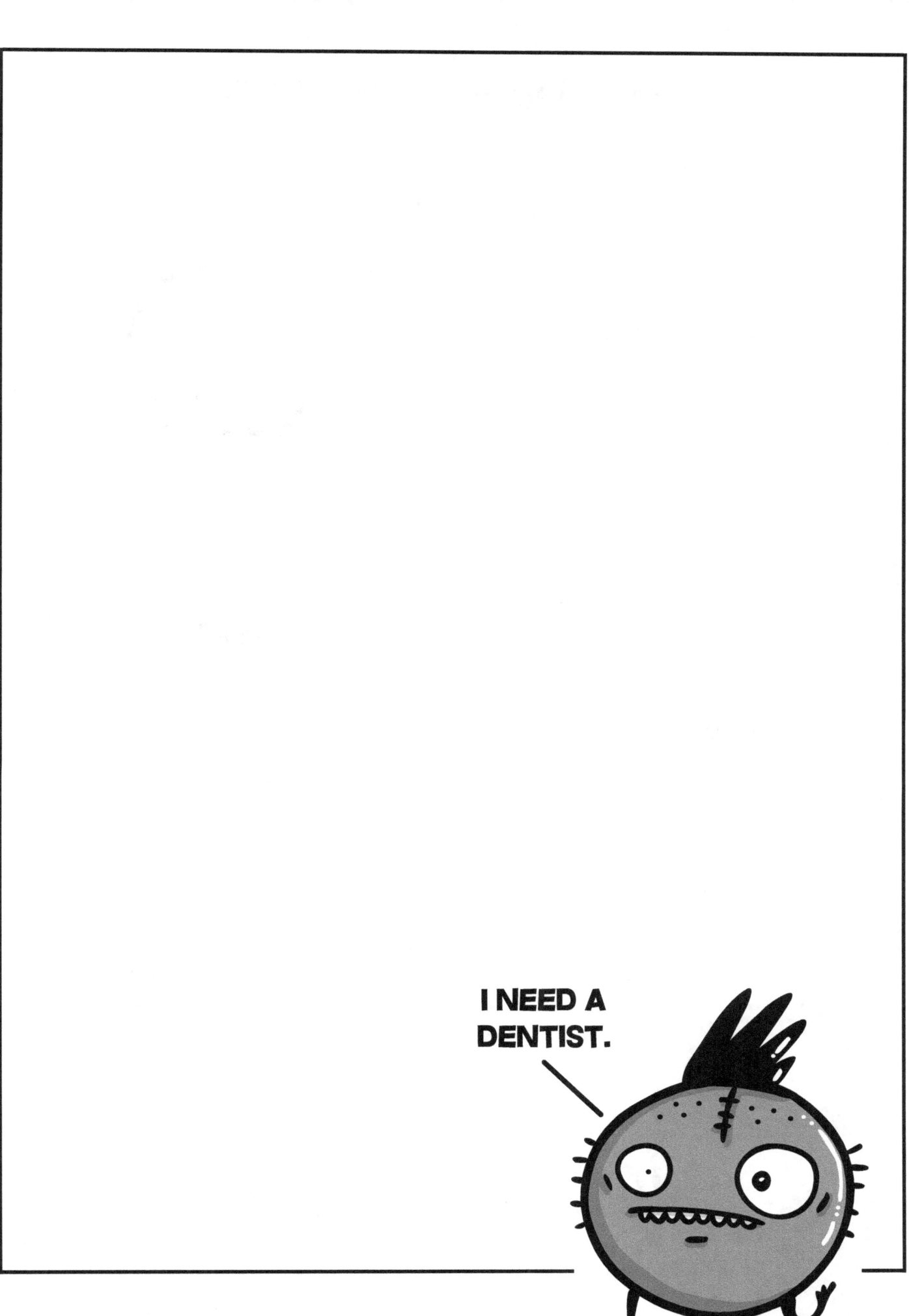

HAHAHA HAPPYCLOUD

1.

2.

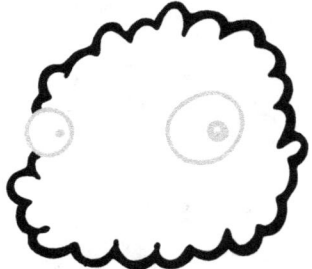

3.

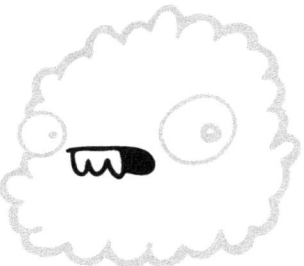

4.

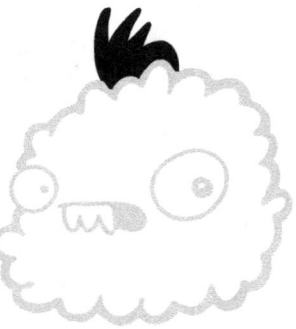

5.

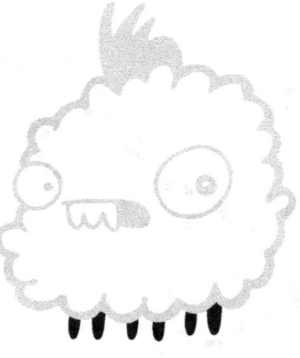

6.

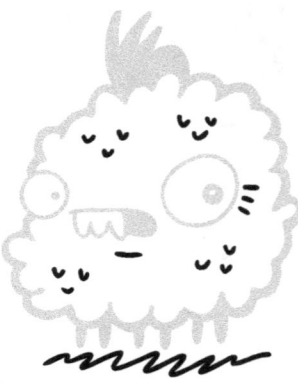

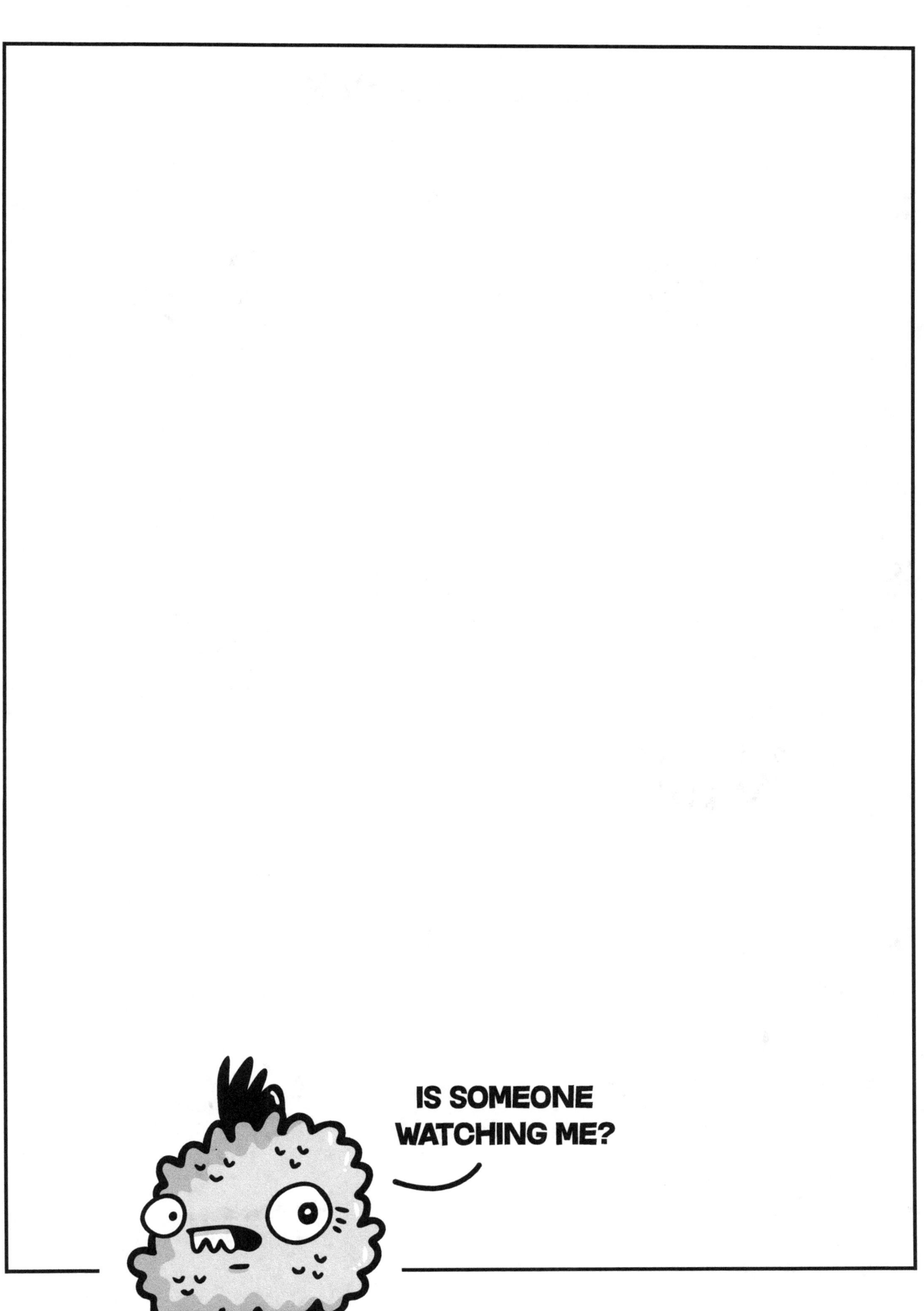

MUDGE WIENER

1.

2.

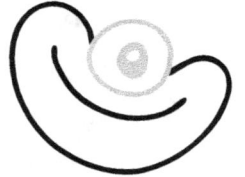

3.

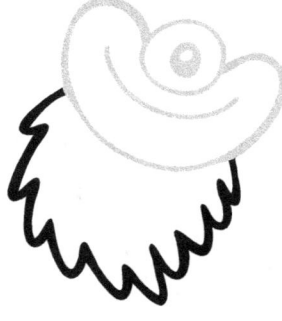

4.

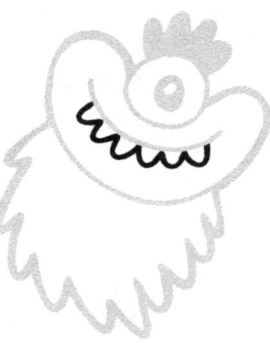

5.

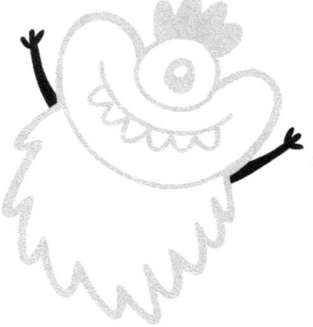

6.

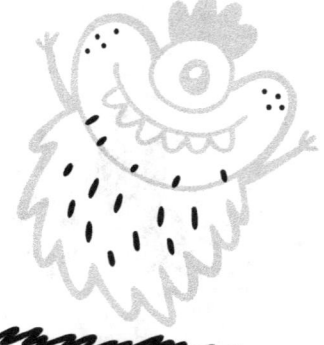

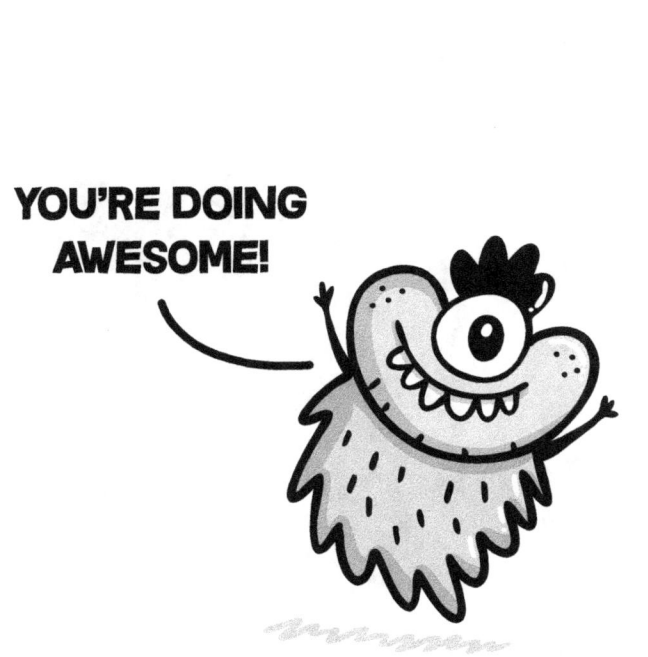

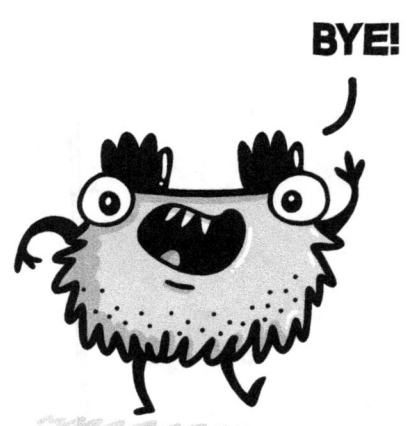